Instructions on Orthodoxy
1964

In the Footsteps of Jesus
1993

By
Archimandrite George Thomas (Thomopoulos)
Tulsa, Oklahoma USA
1998

Light and Life Publishing
P.O. Box 26421
Minneapolis, Minnesota 55426-0421

Copyright © 1998
George Thomas

All rights reserved. No part of this book may be reproduced, stored in a retrieval system, or transmitted in any form or by any means, electronic, mechanical, photocopying, recording, or otherwise without the written permission of Light and Life Publishing.

ISBN 1-880971-37-2

Archimandrite George Thomas (Thomopoulos)

Encyclopedic Synopsis

About the Orthodox Christian Churches of the World from 33 A.D.

Introduction

Part One	Theological
Part Two	Chronological and historical events
Part Three	The Great Separation Between the Western and the Eastern Churches. The Great Schism 1054
Part Four	Protestant Reformation by Martin Luther against Pope of Rome 1517
Part Five	Terminology of the Orthodox Church
Part Six	Calendars Jewish Julian and the Gregorian in 1500
Part Seven	The Greek language in the Christian World. Language of the Holy Gospel. Latin from the 4th Century. Secondary Language to Christianity
Part Eight	Teachers of the Orthodox Church and Administration
Part Nine	Introduction to the Holy Land Pilgrimage
Part Ten	Conclusion, Sources, and Dedication
Part Eleven	Photographic Section

By Archimandrite George Thomas (Thomopoulos)

Tulsa, Oklahoma

Introduction

- Since the day of my retirement, I have devoted all my time in study and research of Christianity including Orthodoxy and other branches of the Christian church.

- I have researched the chronological events from the day of the establishment of the One, Holy, Catholic and Apostolic Church, the teachings, ethos, administration and feast days, and Holy Traditions of the Orthodox Faith.

- The great separation between the Western and Eastern Churches took place in 1054 A.D. We shall discuss the Filique, the protest of Martin Luther against the Pope of Rome and the beginning of the Protestant Reformation in 1517.

- Other subjects we shall discuss in this book are:
  1. The Mormons and their teachings as well as the Jehovah's Witnesses.
  2. The religious calendars: Jewish, Julian, and the Gregorian.
  3. The celebration of the Christian Easter and the Jewish Passover.
  4. The Seven Ecumenical Councils which include teachings and regulations for all churches of the world.
  5. The Greek language as the mother language of Christianity, the language of the Holy Bible throughout the centuries, and the Latin

language as the secondary language of Christianity

6. The Greek language as the language of philology, philosophy, education, civilization and the arts throughout the centuries.

Part One

Theological

According to the Book of Genesis, chapters one and two, we learn that God created the world and all visible and invisible things. He also created human life, Adam and Eve.

As the years passed, people forgot God's original plan and lived in darkness and sin. God sent his prophets to teach and save His people, but they were too far gone. It was very difficult for them to see the light.

Therefore, God wanted to save the world. When the fullness of the time had come, God sent forth his son, made of a woman, made under the law, to redeem them that were under the law, that we might receive the adoption of the Son (Gal. 4:4-5). "For God so loved that world that he gave his only begotten son, that whosoever believeth in him should not perish, but have everlasting life" (John 3:16).

The Coming of the Lord Jesus Christ

The Prophet Isaiah revealed the coming of the Lord in 760 B.C. He prophesied, "Therefore the Lord himself shall give you a sign. Behold, a virgin shall conceive, and bear a Son, and shall call his name Emmanuel" (Isa. 7:14). Isaiah also said, "For unto us a child is born, unto us a son is given and, his name shall be called Wonderful, Counselor, the Mighty God, the everlasting Father, the Prince of Peace" (Isa. 9:6).

The principle sources of information concerning Jesus' life are the Gospels written between 60 and 70 A.D. to facilitate the spread of Christianity throughout the ancient world. All the synoptic gospels of Matthew, Mark and Luke record Jesus' public ministry, beginning after the imprisonment of St. John the Baptist.

All gospels add that for a brief time after His resurrection, Jesus further instructed his disciples in matters pertaining to the Kingdom of God. He also commissioned them to go and teach all nations, baptizing them in the name of the Father, and the Son, and of the Holy Spirit (Matt. 28-19). Finally, according to Luke 24:50-51, he was seen at Bethany to ascend into heaven (Acts 1:2-12). The Ascension occurred forty days after His resurrection.

According to some historians and archaeologists, Jesus was born between 8 and 4 B.C. Jesus is believed by the great majority of Christians to be the incarnate of God and to have been divinely conceived by Mary, the wife of Joseph, a carpenter of Nazareth.

The name Jesus is derived from the Greek, *Christos*, a translation of the Hebrew *Mashiakh*, anointed one or Messiah. The name Christ was used by Jesus' early followers who regarded him as the promised deliverer of Israel. *Christos* or Christ was later made part of Jesus' proper name by the church, which regards him as the redeemer of all mankind.

Chronology of the Writing of the Holy Gospels, Acts, Letters of Saint Paul and the Revelation

- The three synoptic gospels Matthew, Mark and Luke were written between 60-70 A.D.

- The gospel of St. John the Theologian was written in Ephesus, 85-95 A.D

- The Book of Acts was written by the evangelist St. Luke, 70-64 A.D.

- The letters of St. Paul were written between the years of 51-70 A.D

- The Catholic letters of St. Peter were written between 60-66 A.D.

- The Revelation of St. John the Theologian was written in the Island of Patmos in the Aegean Sea in about 95 A.D.

Part Two

History of the Orthodox Church

Origin. The Greek Orthodox Church traces its origin back to the 50th day after the resurrection of our Lord Jesus Christ in the year 33 A.D. This day is universally observed as the Sunday of Pentecost. The word "orthodox" comes from two Greek words, *orthos*, which means true and unchangeable, and, *doxa,* which means glory. Therefore, orthodoxy means true teaching and true worship of God.

Important Historical Dates

The Church is known as the One Holy Catholic and Apostolic Church. The word "catholic" means universal.

A.D.

- 33 Crucifixion, Death, Resurrection and Ascension of our Lord
- 36 Conversion of St. Paul
- 51 St. Paul preaches to the Athenians regarding the Unknown God.
- 52 Apostolic Council of Jerusalem
- 61 The Apostle Peter establishes the Church of Antioch where the faithful were first called Christians
- 64 The first persecution of Christianity by the Roman Emperor Nero. 64-303 A.D., the period of the Great Persecutions.
- 166 Martyrdom of St. Polycarp, Bishop of Smyrna.
- 313 First Ecumenical Council of Nicaea (318

Church Fathers) which condemned the heretic Arius who denied that the Son of God is of one esence with the Father. Formulation of the first seven articles of the Creed.

326   Discovery of the Holy Cross by St. Helen

381   Second Ecumenical Council of Constantinople (186 Church Fathers) which condemned the heretic Macedonius who denied the divinity of the Holy Spirit. Formulation of the final five articles of the Creed.

431   Third Ecumenical Council of Ephesus (200 Church Fathers) which condemned the heretic Nestorius who is the father and founder of Monophysitism; that is to say, he preached that ater the union of the two natures, divine and human, in the person of the Lord Jesus Christ, the human nature was absorbed by the divine, hence his followers were called monophysites. This is in opposition to the Orthodox Church which believes that Jesus Christ was truly God and man, having two natures and two wills.

451   Fourth Ecumenical Council of Chalcedon (630 Church Fathers) which condemned the heretic monophysite Eutyches, who denied that Christ had a true human nature. The human nature, he maintained, was absorbed by the Divine Nature as a drop of wine in the ocean; hence, Christ had only His Divine Nature. This heresy is called, monophysitism from the Greek monos meaning "one" and *physis* "nature."

553   Fifth Ecumenical Council of Constantinople (164 Church Fathers) which condemned: A) The person and writings of Theodore of Mopsuestia, B) The writings of Theodore of Cyrhus against St. Cyril, and C) The letter of Ibas of Edessa to Moris, Bishop of Hardashir of Persia.

657   Fall of Jerusalem to the Arabs

680   The Sixth Ecumenical Council of Constantinople (160 Church Fathers) which condemned the Monothelites who taught that there was one will (Monothelism) in Christ.

787   Seventh Ecumenical Council of Nicaea (368 Church Fathers) which proclaimed that we do not worship icons but we venerate them.

858   Photios the Great becomes Patriarch of Constantinople.

863   Beginning of the Christian mission to the Slavic nations by the Greek monks Methodius and Cyril.

975   The Russians become Orthodox Christians.

1054   Founding of the Roman Catholic Church as a result of the great separation or schism by which the Western and Roman Church broke away from the mother church, the Eastern Orthodox Church.

1099   Fall of Jerusalem to the Crusaders.

1204   Fall of Constantinople to the Crusaders.

1261   Liberation of Constantinople.

1274   The temporary false reunion of the Eastern and Western Church.

1291   Crusaders are forced out of Palestine.

1439 The second temporary false reunion of the Eastern and Western Churches.
1453 Fall of Constantinople to the Turks.
1456 Fall of Athens to the Turks.
1476 Publication of the first printed Greek book, *Greek Grammer* by K. Laskaris.
1517 Beginning of the Protestant Reformation.
1589 Founding of the Russian Patriarchate.
1600 Installation of the Ecumenical Patriarchate in the Fanarion "Fenner" district of Constantinople.
1516 First publication of the Greek New Testament in Europe by Erasmus.
1821 The Greek War of Independence against the Ottoman Empire.
1833 Establishment of the Autcephalous Church of Greece.
1912 Organization of the first Orthodox Sunday school in the United States, Holy Trinity, New York City.
1922 Most Rev. Alexandros, first Greek Orthodox Archbishop in America.
1924 Adoption of the New Calendar by the Greek Church.
1955 Official recognition of the Eastern Orthodox Church as a major faith by the states of West Virginia, Indiana, Delaware, Connecticut, Texas, Pennsylvania and Wisconsin.

Part Three

The Great Separation of West and East - 1054 A.D.

In the beginning of the ninth century, the Western Church added the phrase "and the Son" (filioque) to the Creed. When the bishops of the Eastern Church learned of this addition, they wrote to the bishop or pope of Rome through the patriarch of Constantinople, and communication began regarding this addition to the Creed.

Later, the Greek Fathers of the Church, St. John Chrysostom, St. Basil, Gregorius and others including theologians Marcus, Photius and Eugenius, the bishop of Ephesus, expounded a philosophical and logical analysis of the error of the Western theologians. Still, after all this discussion, the Western Church refused to delete "filioque" from the Creed. From 867 to 1054 many fruitless conferences took place, but the Western theologians unfortunately refused to go back to the teachings of the first and second synods on this point, even though they had accepted it from the beginning. This dogmatic error stands to this date in the Roman Catholic Church.

The Western or Roman Catholic Church broke away from the mother church (the Eastern Orthodox Church) in 1054 A.D. From the beginning up to 1054, the Orthodox Church never used the word "orthodox" but was known as one with the rest of the Christian churches of the world.

Thus, the Western Church was cut off from the other four branches Constantinople, Alexandria, Antioch and Jerusalem, which are united to this day.

When the Western Church added to the Creed the phrase "and the Son" instead of "from the Father" as originally was adopted, then the Eastern church accepted the word Orthodox which means "unchangeable."

Part Four

The Protestant Reformation 1517

The last period begins in the year 1517 A.D. when the Protestant Reformation begins. The Eastern Orthodox Church had nothing to do with the separation of the Protestants from the Catholic Church.

Language

The early Christians used the Greek language in the Eastern and Western Empire, except in Egypt and Asia where Arabic was used. The Church of Rome was also Greek and the first missionaries to France and England were Greeks from Asia Minor.

Latin was used in Rome after Jerome translated the Old and New Testaments into Latin from the Hebrew and Greek. Therefore, we see that Latin became the official language of the Roman Catholic Church at about the fourth century A.D.

Up to the end of the third century in the Church of Rome, the liturgy was chanted in the Greek language. Later, at the beginning of the fourth century, St. Ambrosios began using the Latin liturgy still using hymns from the Greek Church. St. Ambrosios excluded the organ and he consecrated the Eastern Antiphon Song and imposed the four master tones. During the first few centuries of Christianity, Rome was the missionary outpost of the West, and her bishops and priests were mostly Greeks.

Administration and Population of the Eastern Orthodox Church

The Eastern Orthodox Church is also known as the Greek Orthodox Church and is administered by four patriarchs: Jerusalem, Antioch, Alexandria and Constantinople.

The patriarch of Constantinople is known as the Ecumenical Patriarch and is recognized as first among equals by the other three patriarchs. He is the spiritual leader of the 300 million Orthodox throughout the world.

Establishment of Jesuits in Ninth Century. Greek Catholic Church in Poland

A religious order of men in the Roman Catholic Church was founded by Ignatius of Loyola in 1543. The motto of the Jesuit Order is "Ad majoreum Dei Corian" to "the Greater Glory of God." Long preparation involving many years of study is required of a candidate for this order.

Historically, the aim of Ignatius of Loyola in forming his order was to convert the Muslims. But due to the outbreak of war with the Ottoman Turks, they asked the pope to do missionary work in other parts of the world. Missions were established by Francis Xavier in India, Japan, China and Africa.

1872 Jehovah's Witnesses

Jehovah's Witnesses is a Christian sect founded in 1872 in Pittsburgh, Pennsylvania by the American clergyman Charles Taze Russell. The sect maintains a large publishing house that prints books and pamphlets in many languages. Its best known periodical, The Watch Tower, is printed in 74 languages. In the late 1960s, the world membership of active adherents numbered about 1,160,000 in the United States of America.

Mormons 1830

The Mormons are a religious organization known officially as the Church of Jesus Christ of Later Day Saints. The group was founded in 1830 by an American Joseph Smith, who in the same year published the book of Mormon. In July 1847, Brigham Young and 148 pioneers reached the valley of the Great Salt Lake in Utah where he founded a Mormon settlement.

Mormons' Doctrines

The articles of faith of the Church of Jesus Christ of Later Day Saints include the following:

- We believe in God, the Eternal Father, and His Son Jesus Christ, and the Holy Ghost.

- We believe that men will be punished for their own sins and not Adam's transgression.

- We believe that the first principles and ordinances of the gospel are 1) Faith in the Lord Jesus Christ, 2) Repentance 3) Baptism by immersion for the remission of sins, 4) Laying on the hands for the gifts of the Holy Ghost.

- We believe the Bible to be the work of God, as far as it is translated correctly. We also believe the book of Mormon to be the word of God.

- Lastly, we believe that the City of Salt Lake, Utah, is the New Jerusalem.

Part Five

Terminology of the Orthodox Faith.
Sources of the Orthodox Church.

There are eight sources divided into two headings:
1. Holy Scriptures
2. Sacred Tradition

Holy Scriptures comprise (1) Old Testament as translated in Alexandria in the third century B.C. from the Hebrew into the Greek by 70 (some say 72) outstanding scholars of that day and (2) the original version of the New Testament which was written in Greek between 60 to 90 A.D.

Sacred Tradition includes:
1. Holy Baptism
2. Chrismation - Confirmation
3. Holy Eucharist - Holy Communion
4. Confession

All of the above are compulsory

5. Holy Orders - Ordination
6. Holy Matrimony - Marriage
7. Holy Unction - Efhelaion

These three are non-compulsory

For Daily Service we have
1. Vespers
2. Evening prayer (Compline Apodipon)
3. Midnight Service (Meso-Nyktikon)
4. Matins (Orthos)
5. Divine Liturgy

The Holy Orders are three
1. Deacon
2. Priest (Presbyteros)
3. Bishop

Bishops go under different titles:
1. Auxiliary Bishop (assistant to the archbishop)
2. Metropolitan
3. Archbishop, and
4. Patriarch

As for terms and titles we use the following:
1. Catholic (a Greek word meaning universal)
2. Preacher
3. Sermon
4. Doxology
5. Movable & fixed holy days
6. Missionary
7. Chancellor
8. Dean
9. Priest
10. Monk
11. Nun
12. Proselyte
13. Canter (Psaltis)
14. Icon
15. Fasting (lent)
16. Memorial service (Mnemosynon)

Divine Liturgy and its Parts

Definition: Divine Liturgy comes from the Greek words, *Ergon* and *Laos*. It means the work of the people. It is a sacrament. It is a mystical action between God and man.

In the Orthodox faith we have daily services consisting of (a) Vesper Service, (b) Matins (Orthros), and (c) Divine Liturgy.

(a) Vesper Service

It is compulsory to perform the Vesper Service every Saturday night or the night before holy days. The purpose of the Vesper service is to prepare the clergy and laity for the service of the next morning. The service consists of psalms, hymns, prophecies, petitions and dismissal hymn.

(b) Orthros

Orthros means "upon sunrise." The early Christians went to the church before beginning their daily work to offer prayers by performing the Orthros. The Orthros consists of psalms, hymns, readings, petitions, praises and doxology. Orthros is altogether separate from the Divine Liturgy.

(c) Divine Liturgy (Prothesis)

Between Orthros and Divine Liturgy the priest prepares the Holy Gifts, as we say in Greek the *"Prothesis,"* which means "first place" or "preparation." The place where he prepares the Holy Gifts signifies the manger of Bethlehem where Christ was born. The Divine Liturgy starts from the beginning

of the life of Christ. Therefore, we divide the Divine Liturgy into three parts:
1. Remembrance
2. Sacrifice
3. Communion

(1) Remembrance:

It is a remembrance of the life, the cross, the burial, and the resurrection of our Lord. As we read in the Bible, "Do ye this in remembrance of me" (Luke 22:19; Cor. 11:24-25).

(2) Sacrifice:

It is a sacrifice, "This is my body which is broken for you. This is my blood which is shed for you and many others" (Matt. 26:26-28; Mark 14:22-23; Luke 22:19-209, 1 Cor. 11:24-25).

(3) Communion:

"Take and eat, drink of it ye all" (Matt. 26:26-27). The whole drama of the Divine Liturgy can be divided in six parts:
1. Petition
2. Small Entrance
3. Great Entrance
4. Anaphora
5. Communion
6. Dismissal

Forms of the Divine Liturgy

In the Eastern Orthodox Faith we have five liturgies:

1. St. James (Iakovos)
2. St. Mark
3. St. Basil's
4. St. John Chrysostom
5. Presanctified Gifts.

The first liturgy of St. Iakovos was written by the first ordained bishop of Jerusalem. It is a long service that is performed once a year on the feast day of St. James (Iakovos) on October 23.

St. Mark's liturgy is observed only in Alexandria, Egypt, once a year, on St. Mark's Day, April 25.

St. Basil wrote his Divine Liturgy by eliminating some of the prayers from the Iakovos Liturgy. St. Basil's liturgy is performed ten times annually, i.e., the first five Sundays of Lent, Holy Thursday, Holy Saturday, the day before Christmas, New Year's Day, and the day before Epiphany.

St. John Chrysostom wrote a shorter Divine Liturgy which is performed all year except for the above mentioned dates.

The Liturgy of the Presanctified Gifts or the Apostolic Liturgy, as it was called for the first 200 years after Christ, is performed every Wednesday and Friday of Lent; also on Monday, Tuesday, and Wednesday of Holy Week. It is a silent liturgy and we call it prescanctified because we do not prepare gifts, as we do in the other liturgies. The gifts are blessed on the previous Sunday.

Mass vs. Liturgy

In the Orthodox faith, we do not use the word "mass." We use the work liturgy. Mass comes from the Latin phrase "messa-est" which means "it has been offered."

Orthodox Churches Throughout the World

The Orthodox churches through their missionaries founded churches in Russia, Georgia, Yugoslavia, Romania, Poland, Bulgaria, Albania, Mt. Sinai and later on in Finland, Czechoslovakia, Estonia, Latvia, Lithuania, China and Japan. All the above churches were and continue to be independent of each other in administrative matters. Although the local language is used in each of these churches, they all follow the same faith. They share the same liturgies and services that were handed down by the ancient churches of the first centuries and transmitted to the nations of Europe, Africa and Asia. All these Orthodox churches are united by the same undivided and sacred tradition and comprise the most democratic religious body in the world. And, all are under the jurisdiction of the Greek Ecumenical Patriarch of Constantinople.

Part Six

Calendars
Jewish - Julian - Gregorian 1500

From the beginning of time we have had six calendars.

A. The Jewish calendar was known as Years of Jacob.

This calendar was known to us through the Old Testament. When Abraham left the city of Shur and went west to Geras, he took this calendar with him. This calendar consisted of twelve circles. Before Exodus the number twelve was a holy one. The zodiac system was used for the twelve sons of Jacob.

Genesis: Chapter 49

1. Issachar	for	Taurus
2. Reubin	for	Aquarius
3. Zabulun	for	Pisces
4. Nephtali	for	Capricorn
5. Joseph	for	Sagittarius
6. Dan	for	Scorpio
7. Asher	for	Libra
8. Judah	for	Leo
9. Benjamin	for	Cancer
10. Gad	for	Aries
11. Simeon & Levi	for	Gemini
12. Sina, Jacob's daughter	for	Virgo

Twelve sons of Jacob - Twelve Tribes - Twelve hours of the day - Twelve doors in the Holy City of Jerusalem and later Twelve disciples of Christ. After Exodus, the number seven was added also as a holy number.

B. The Egyptian Calendar

C. The Babylonian Calendar - 3000 B.C.

D. The Greek Calendar

E. The Julian Calendar by Julius Caesar

F. The Gregorian Calendar by Pope of Rome, Gregory XIII

Rome was built in 753 B.C. Later in the year 46 B.C, which is 708 years later, Julius Caesar brought to Rome the Greek astronomers, Sosi-Gens and Marcus Fabius to invent a new calendar for him. They invented the calendar known as the Julian.

During the days of Christ and up the 15th century, the Julian calendar was used by all Christians. Easter was celebrated according to the Julian calendar. The beginning of Easter goes back to the Egyptians who celebrated the vernal equinox because the day begins to become longer than the night. The light overcomes the darkness. This celebration was called Pisah, from the Greek verb Piso, which means passage of the sun through the equator. "Light over darkness or darkness behind light."

The Jewish celebration signifies passage of the Red Sea, freedom from slavery, and hope for salvation. This celebration is called Pessach or Pascha.

The first day of the month of Nisan was the day of the vernal equinox. The tenth day up to the fourteenth of the same month, each family must have been supplied with a male lamb and they kept it up to the fourteenth day of the same month. In the evening of the fourteenth day of the full moon, which is the first day after the vernal equinox, they sacrificed the lamb in the Holy Temple (Exodus 12:3-11).

So the Jewish people celebrated Easter or Passover on the fourteenth day of the month of Nisan. The Christians celebrated in the same month, but always on a Sunday. Now as the Easter or Pascha of the Christians sometimes coincided with the Passover of the Jews, and because it was thought to be unChristian to celebrate such an important festival at the same time as the Jews did, Constantine the Great called the first Ecumenical Synod of Nicaea in the year 325 A.D. which formulated the following rule which was accepted by all Christians:

The Christian Pascha or Easter will always be celebrated on Sunday following the first full moon after the vernal equinox, which was then to take place on March 21, according to the Julian calendar. If the full moon will take place on any day of the week except Sunday, or if it is on Sunday, Easter will be celebrated on the following Sunday. This celebration will be between March 22 and no later than April 25 on the Julian calendar, or March 22 to May 8 on the Gregorian calendar, never before the Jewish Passover. The full moon will be based according to the Julian calendar and not the Gregorian calendar.

This resolution was in practice until the fifteenth century. In the year 1582, the pope of Rome, Gregory the XIII adopted another calendar known as Gregorian calendar. He added 13 days to the Julian calendar. Therefore October 4, 1582, became October 17, 1582. He also changed the date of the Easter celebration according to his Gregorian calendar. Thus, he overlooked the rule regarding the celebration of the Jewish Passover. The Gregorian calendar was also adopted by the Protestant faith in 1700 A.D., the church of England in 1752 A.D., the church of Greece on March 10, 1924, and Communist Russia on Feb. 14, 1918.

The Church of Greece and the United States celebrate all the feast days of the Ecclesiastical year according to the Gregorian calendar except Pascha (Easter), which is celebrated according to the Julian calendar. Pascha or Pessach comes from the Greek verb *Pascho*, meaning to suffer or to feel pain. The Jews suffered in slavery, Christ suffered and felt pain, and was in agony before victory came. The word Easter does not express the true meaning of Pascha. Easter comes from two Greek words - East or *Anatoli* and star *Astro*. Star gives light and light comes from the East. Also Pascha means suffer at first and victory at last—pain and joy—death and resurrection. According to St. John, Chapter 12, verse 1, "Then Jesus, six days before the Feast of the Passover," celebrated the Jewish Passover with his disciples and was crucified after the celebration.

To this day, the Orthodox Church keeps and follows all rules and regulations from the beginning of the Christian Church on Pentecost and does not accept any changes or additions unless they come from the whole body of the church - Ecumenical or Catholic - Universal.

Music:

The Ecclesiastical music goes back to the Jewish Psalmodies of the Old Testament. From Exodus: 1-19, we learn that every time the people of Israel were in trouble and were freed by God, they praised the Lord with their voices and instruments. The same can be found in the book of the Prophet Isaiah 13:20.

Part Seven

The Greek and Latin Languages in the Christian Faith

Greek Language
Grammatical and Pronunciation

Greek is an Indo-European language using twenty-four letters in the alphabet.

In ancient times the Greeks used two more letters, the American F and the letter J. The letter F was called digammon. The letter J was pronounced like IO. Xenophon, an ancient Greek writer in his book *Kyrou Anabasis* used the letter F in place of two gamma, the digamon - parasafas - parasangs - phalafas - phalagas. The letter J - IO was used by the Attic dialect in the duel and especial in the political speeches.

The Greek alphabet is divided in two parts. Seventeen consonants and seven vowels. The vowels are A, E, H, I, O, Y and W. Eight diphthongs are created by using the seven vowels. The diphthongs are A+I==E—E+I. O+I+-Y+I and OY=OO Look. Also, we have A+Y=AV or AF. EY==EV or IF==HY==HB or IF and O+Y==OO=Book.

The Greek language has three genders: arsenikon - thylikon - ouderteron - masculine - femine - and nueter ==o=the==to-the Father - the mother and the child has five cases. They are onomastiki - geniki - dotiki - aitiatiki and klhtiki == nominative - genitive - dative - accustaive - and vocative. Two numbers — enikos+ plhthyntikos-singular-plural. The dual number was used in ancient times DY - I. Kos ....

The use of the Greek language on the Greek mainland goes back to the early second millennium B.C.

Modern Greek grew out of the popular Byzantine language, which in turn stemmed from the common language *Koini* used throughout the Greek world at the time of Alexander the Great.

Turkish, Slavic, Albanian, Italian and French words enriched the idiom. They spoke from the language DE-MO-TI-KI. Demotic has become a rich and forceful literary medium.

Next, we will speak about the historical and prehistoric Greek language from 1000 B.C. Mediterranean people, closely akin to the races of Northern Africa, inhabited the Southern Aegean area as far back as the Neolithic age, before 4000 B.C. from the Stone Age to the Bronze Age. The Bronze Age civilization flourished in the Aegean after 3000 B.C. and was divided into two main cultures each of which passed through several subdivisions.

One centered on the Island of Crete, only 400 miles northwest of Egypt and directly on the sea routes to the ancient countries of the Middle East. Cretan culture is called Minoan (from *Minos*, the generic name for the Cretan kings). The other culture, called Helladic, flourished contemporaneously on the mainland of Greece, particularly in the Peloponnisos. Its greatest centers were at Mycenae Tiryns (near present Navplion and Pylos). Cretan culture and trade dominated the Mediterranean until almost 1500 B.C. when leadership passed to the mainland Greeks.

Ancient Greek Language

The ancient Greek language was in use for centuries before the era of recorded history. Prehistoric people migrated from central and northern Asia to the more fertile lands to the south. They settled in various sections of Greece and a unique dialect arose in each: 1. Arcado-Cyprian, 2. Doric, 3. Aeolic, and 4. Ionic.

1. Arcado-Cyprian is a dialect about which very little is known. It is the descendant of a form spoken in Mycenean time in the Peloponnese and some of the southern islands. Excavations made in Crete and on the mainland of Greece after 1900 B.C., revealed it as ancestor (1500-1400 B.C.) of Arcado-Cyprian. These researchers indicated that the Greeks were a literate people, many hundreds of years before the period of the first Greek poet Homer.

2. The Doric dialect, originally spoken in northern Greece, largely supplanted the Arcado- Cyprian dialect in the Peloponnese and came to be spoken also in the southern Cyclades, on the island of Crete, and also in the Greek colonies in Asia Minor, Sicily and Italy. Most of the poems of Theocritus were written in this dialect, and the language of Pindar has many traits found in Doric.

3. Aeolic was spoken principally in the district of Aeolis, Thessalia and Boeotia. It was the language used by the poets Alcaeus and Sappho, and three of Idys of Theocritus.

4. The Ionic dialect was spoken on many of the islands of the Aegean and on most of the western shore of Asia Minor. It was employed in various

literary works of the fifth century B.C. notably the writings of the physician Hippocrates and the historian Herodotus. The language of the Homeric poems is the deposit of a literary tradition that seems to have begun in the Mycenaean, came down through Aeolic and Ionic, and was given final shape in Attic. The largest element in it is Ionic. From the Ionic dialect developed the Attic, the standard form of classical Greek. It was the language of Athens and the surrounding district of Attica, and differed from the other ionic forms chiefly in its construction of vowels. Because of the political supremacy of Athens during and after the fifth century B.C. and the dominant role of Athenian art, philosophy and drama, the Attic dialect superseded all others and became the chief literary language. Its influence was enhanced through its use by the greatest contemporary intellects including the playwrights Aeschylus, Euripides, and Sophocles, the orator Demosthenes, the philosopher Plato, and the historians Thucydides and Xenophon. During the fourth century B.C. with the conquests of Alexander the Great, there was a shift in the population from Greece proper to the new Greek colonies in the Middle East.

In this period, known as the Hellenistic, the Attic dialect, spoken by the educated as well as by the merchants and many emigrants, became the language common to all the Middle East. As the Greeks mixed with other people, linguistic changes took place. Attic became the foundation of a new form of Greek, Koine, which spread throughout all areas of Greek influence. Koine was the language of the court, and of literature and commerce throughout the Hellenistic empire. Koine soon became differentiated into two groups, literary Koine and vernacular, or the popular tongue. The literary language was spoken and used by the educated upper classes, who until the Roman Conquest, maintained a vigorous and independent intellectual and artistic life while not forgetting great writers of earlier times.

The vernacular tongue, on the other hand, was less influenced either by classical reminiscences or by the new developments of Hellenistic thought. It borrowed more freely from the vocabularies of middle eastern languages and suffered more severely from breakdown of the traditional grammar. It is known mainly from letters and documents on papyrus, and only slowly came to be used in literary works by lower-class writers. Of these, the most important are the four gospels, which, however, show a peculiar form of Koine with strong Semitic admixture. Later church fathers wrote in the literary language.

During the first and second centuries A.D., a group of scholars advocated a return to the pure Attic dialect of the fifth and fourth centuries BC. Despite the vigorous support of the philosopher Galen and the grammarian Phrynicus (second century A.D.) and the brilliant use of the dialect by such writers as Lucian, the so-called Atticist movement was not wholly successful. Many great writers of the second century and later including the essayist and biographer Plutarchus and the geographer Pausanias (138-180 A.D.) used the literary Koine but Atticists also continued to rise and occasionally dominated the literary scene. As the Byzantine Empire broke up, its territory became divided into small independent states. The literary Koine, which was confined to the great cultural centers, remained static, but the vernacular Koine broke up into many local dialects, developing further as it was influenced by the mirating peoples in the Middle East; the Venetians, Turks, Bulgarians, and Albanians among others. The Balkans meanwhile gradually became isolated from the great naval and commercial enterprises of Western Europe, which was becoming concerned with the New World.

Modern Greek. Throughout the Byzantine period and the years of Turkish domination, the Greek Literary language remained largely static. The main literature produced was hagiography, theological works, and religious poetry. In Greece proper, which remained under Ottoman Turkish rule, the energies of the people were absorbed by revolutionary activities aimed at national independence. After the Greek liberation of 1821, the leaders of this widespread movement were known as Demotikists because the vernacular language is called Demotike. Prominent among such advocates were the poet Dionysios Solomos (1798-1857) and the French philologist of Greek descent Jean Psiharis (1854-1929). Later, the leading scholars such as professors of philology at the University of Athens accepted the scholarly Katharevousa for all official speeches, correspondence and publication, and made it compulsory in all schools. It is also the language of the Greek court and of most newspapers.

The principal grammatical differences between modern and ancient Greek are in declension and verbal conjugation. Two basic forms are used in ancient Greek: dual, a form indicating that a noun, pronoun, or adjective refers to two persons or things, and the dative case, which is used only in a few idiomatic expressions. Modern Greek makes extensive use of auxiliary verbs. The ancient Greek imperative forms have been largely supplanted by the use of an auxiliary with the subjunctive form of the verb. In vocabulary, modern Greek vernacular is characterized by the use of a large number of words borrowed directly from foreign languages, especially from Italian, Turkish, and French, and by a great facility for combining words.

Greek Literature. Literature of the Greek-speaking people from about the end of the second millennium B.C. until the present developed as a national expression with little outside influence until the Hellenistic period, and had a formative effect upon all succeeding European literature.

Greek Art and Architecture. Arts and architecture of Greece and the Greek colonies from about 1100 B.C. to the first century B.C. emphasize the dynamic aspects of living forms. Its primary subject matter is the human form, which is used to represent both humans and gods.

Latin Language
Rome 753 B.C.

Rome, founded according to tradition in 753 B.C., produced no real literature in the first 500 years of history. Few fragments survive on the early beginning of poetry, epitaphs, and religious songs, prose, speeches and legal writing.

In the third century B.C. the Romans were brought into close contact with the Greeks of southern Italy and Sicily and for the first time became acquainted with Greek poetry and drama.

Latin language was not native to Italy, but was brought into the Italian peninsula in prehistoric times by Italic people who migrated from the north. A member of the Italic sub-family of the family of Indo-European language, it is related to Sankskrit and the Greek and to the Germanic and Celtic tongues.

Development of the Latin literary language may be divided into four periods, corresponding in general to the periods of Latin literature. The early period, 240-70 B.C., includes the writings of Quintus Ennis, Tito Macious Plautus, and Publius Terentus Afer, usually called Terrence.

The Golden Age (14 to 130 A.D.) is characterized by a striving both for historical elaboration and ornament and for concise and epigrammatic expression. The later qualities are found especially in the works of the philosopher and dramatist Lucius Annaeus Seneca and the historian Publius Cornileus Tacitus.

The late Latin period extends from the second century to the sixth century A.D. (about 636) and includes the patristic Latin of the early Christian church. During the third and fourth centuries, the most active writers were Christian apologists, notably, Quintus Septimius, Floren Tertillianius, Saint Ambrosius, Lucius Coelius, Lectantius, and Fermianus known respectively as Tertullian, Saint Ambrosius and Lactantius, and Saint Jerome, who translated the Holy Bible into Latin.

Saint Augustine whose "Confessions" and "Civitate - City of God" are among the greatest literary works of the late empire.

Latin remained the language of pedagogy, diplomacy and scholarship in western Europe throughout the Middle Ages. The Renaissance religious, philosophical, and scientific works were written in Latin, as was much of the poetry, such as the enlogues and epistles of the Italian poet Petrach and the Latin "Elegies" of the English poet John Milton.

Orthodox Churches in the United States and Canada

The first Greek Orthodox Church in the United States was established in 1864 in New Orleans. By 1906, another nineteen churches were established and the number of Orthodox churches continued to grow.

In North and South America, there are now two and a half million communicants under the jurisdiction of the Greek Archdiocese with headquarters in New York City.

Archbishop Iakovos (1993) had 10 bishops as his assistants. Dioceses were located in New York City; Boston; Chicago; Pittsburgh; Los Angeles; Detroit; Houston; Charlotte, North Carolina; Denver; Montreal, Canada; Buenos Aires and South America.

The Greek Archdiocese has under her jurisdiction 500 churches, 540 clergymen, 370 chapters of Philoptochos Women's Societies, 459 Greek parochial schools with 498 Greek teachers, 19,000 students, 414 Sunday schools with 4,036 teachers and 46,495 children. The Greek Theological School was established in 1937. St. Basil's Academy was established in 1944. The Greek Orthodox Youth of America (GOYA) has headquarters in the Greek Archdiocese in New York. The archbishop is their spiritual leader.

Part Eight

Teachings and Administration On the Orthodox Faith

The Orthodox Church teaches that:

1. There are three Divine Persons in God, distinct, yet equal.

2. The Father is neither begotten, nor proceeds from anyone.

3. The Son is begotten from the Father, of the very essence of the Father. He is God and also truly man like us, because He assumed human nature from the Blessed Virgin Mary, except for sin. He died on the cross to save mankind and He ascended into heaven. He will come again "to judge the living and the dead."

4. The Holy Spirit proceeds from the Father.

5. The world is not self-created but is the work of one God.

The Eastern Orthodox Church also teaches that:
1. There are seven sacraments:
a. Baptism
b. Confirmation or Chrismation
c. Holy Eucharist
d. Confession
e. Ordination
f. Marriage

g. Holy Unction.

2. That no one can be saved unless he/she is baptized.

3. That the Holy Scriptures and Sacred Tradition are of equal value and that they complete each other.

4. That God assigned to every person an angel to help him/her.

5. That after death, man's body goes to earth, and the soul which is immortal is presented before God, and according to its actions, pre-enjoys happiness or pre-suffers punishment until the General Judgment.

6. That of all saints, the Mother of God has a supreme grace and that the veneration given to icons and relics relates not to the sacred images as such, but to the person whom they represent.

7. That God knows which road man will take, but he does not predestine him.

Part Nine

Introduction
Pilgrimage to the Holy Land

The Land of Israel is the crossroads of ancient civilization. It is the land of the Bible and the cradle of the three monotheistic religious. This land is holy for Jews, Christians and Moslems. A visit to Israel is a journey back into earliest history, a pilgrimage to the very source of faith.

It is the land of the patriarchs, buried in Hebron; the land of Moses, who on Mt. Sinai received the Ten Commandments; of Elijah, who confounded the idolaters on Mt. Carmel; of Isaiah and Jeremiah and the prophets who spoke the word of God. It is the land of the kings of Israel: David, who made Jerusalem his capital, and Solomon his son, who built the first temple there.

It is the land of Jesus: Bethlehem, where he was born, and where on Christmas Eve, the Midnight Liturgy takes place in the Church of the Nativity, built above the sacred manger; Nazareth, Cana, Mount Tabor, the Jordan River, the Sea of Galilee with Tabgha and Capernaum, and the Mount of the Beatitudes. And finally the culmination of it all, the core of the Holy Land, the eternal city of Jerusalem, encompassing the Church of the Holy Sepulcher and the Garden Tomb, the Via Dolorosa, the Garden of Gethsemane on the Mount of Olives and the upper room of the Last Supper on Mount Zion.

On Mount Moriah, the Temple Mount, stand two of Islam's most holy shrines, the Dome of the Rock and the Mosque of El Aqsa. Here also is Judaism's holiest shrine of all, the Western Wall, all that remains of the ancient temple.

Archaeological remains throughout the country bear witness to its glorious and stormy history and to the domination of successive conquerors. Biblical, Hellenistic and Roman cities, impressive second and third century synagogues and Byzantine churches with fine mosaic floors, Crusader towns and fortresses, Ottoman Walls, and the Dead Sea scrolls, a Hebrew manuscript record discovered after 2,000 years in the caves of Qumran.

A pilgrimage to the Holy Land is an invitation to walk in the footsteps of Jesus.

Sea of Galilee

The Sea of Galilee or Gennesaret, is in a region where Jesus spent much of His life. It was the focal point of His activities during the ministry in Galilee. Here Jesus calmed the stormy waters upon whose surface He walked. The miracle of the abundant catch of fish also occurred here, and to this day the fresh waters of the Sea of Galilee still teem with fish.

Capernaum

This lakeside village on the shore of the Sea of Galilee is referred to frequently in the New Testament as a center of Jesus' ministry. It was the home of many of His disciples, notably Peter. Capernaum abounds with reminders of Jesus' activities. Its ancient synagogue recalls the fact that Jesus used to teach in the synagogue at Capernaum.

Magdala

Magdala is the home of Mary Magdalene. Magdala was a Roman settlement located on an important junction of an ancient trade route. Archaeological excavation here revealed remains of paved streets, a villa, a swimming pool and a building thought to be a synagogue.

Tiberias

Tiberias was established by Herod Antipas between 17 and 22 B.C. as the capital of Galilee and Perea. Tiberias was named after the Emperor Tiberius. It is the site of a Crusader and Turkish stronghold as well as an important site of Jewish pilgrimage.

The tombs of leading Jewish sages, including those of the great medieval rabbi, philosopher and physician Maimonides and of Rabbi Meir Baal Ha'ness and Rabbi Yochanan ben Zakkai are situated here.

Hammath

Hammath is a fortified city of the tribe of Naphtali, and one of Solomon's store cities. It is renowned since the Roman period for its hot springs.

Tabgha

This is the site of the miracle of the multiplication of loaves and fish. Commemorated by the church of the multiplication which is constructed over a fish mosaic dating from a Byzantine basilica of the fifth century. The Church of Primacy, which is also situated here, contains a large rock called the Mensa Christ or the table of Christ upon which Jesus shared a meal with his disciples. It was at this spot that Jesus delegated the primacy of the church to Peter, commissioning him to be the shepherd of Christ's flock, according to Roman Catholic teaching.

Bethsaida

This is the native residence of the apostles where Philip, Simon, and Andrew. Jesus fed the 5,000 and healed the blind man.

The Mount of Beatitudes
The Beatitudes

The Central core of Christ's preaching is to be found in the three chapters of the gospel known as the Sermon on the Mount, Matt. 5-7. The mount itself is situated close to Tabgha, although the Church of the Beatitudes, which commemorates the Sermon on the Mount, lies slightly to the west. It was on the Mount of the Beatitudes that Jesus chose the Twelve Apostles.

Nain

This is the town of the tribe of Issacher, at whose gates Jesus raised the widow's only son from the dead.

Cana

This town has not changed much outwardly since the times of Jesus when he turned water into wine at the wedding celebration. Cana is the birthplace of the apostle Bartholomew or Nathanael.

Mount Tabor

Mount Tabor constitutes a natural stronghold towering over the fertile Jezreel Valley and affords an unforgettable view. It was here that Deborah and Barak defeated Sisera's army as is recalled in the victory song of Deborah in the Old Testament. But the chief significance of Mount Tabor lies in the fact that it was the site of the transfiguration of Jesus, linking him directly to Moses and Elijah.

On this imposing height, looking down on the Jezreel Valley where Gideon gathered his 300 warriors, the disciples saw their Master in his glorious splendor (Matt. 17:1-3).

Not far from here, Saul consulted the witch of Endor (Sam. 28:7). Across the valley, at the foot of Mount Gilboa is Bet She'san upon whose walls were hung the bodies of Saul and Jonathan, slain by the Philistines (Sam. 31:10).

Mount Carmel and Megiddo

To beautiful Mount Carmel came King Saul (Sam. 15:12) and here King Ahab gathered all Israel to witness the confrontation between Elijah and the idol worshippers, including the 450 prophets of Baal and the 400 prophets of the grove (1 Kings 18:19).

Nazareth

Nazareth was Jesus' childhood home, where he studied and worked, forging the theories that would shape the years to come. Jesus was nevertheless forced to leave Nazareth after his teachings estranged him from his townspeople.

Nazareth has been inhabited since biblical times, although no mention is made of it in the Old Testament. Its history was marked by successive cycles of destruction and renewal, and Christian residence in the town was prohibited following its devastation at the hands of Sultan Belbars in 1263 until the seventeenth century. The character of Nazareth has changed little over the years. Its plentiful fruit trees, vineyards and fields breathe an almost biblical tranquility. Most of the holy sites are centrally located and may be covered on foot.

The Basilica of the Annunciation

The largest church in the Middle East stands over the grotto where the Angel Gabriel announced the forthcoming birth of Jesus to Mary. The fifth church to stand on this spot, it incorporates remains of previous churches and is richly adorned with mosaics and gifts from all over the world.

The Church of our Lady's Fear is the place where Mary watched Jesus being pursued by his adversaries after His preaching was unfavorably received in the synagogue. In order to escape, Jesus leapt over a precipice.

The Greek Catholic Church of the Old Synagogue is supposedly the site of the synagogue where Jesus preached and worshipped before becoming estranged from his townspeople and his subsequent departure.

Mary's Well, located to the north of the Basilica of the Annunciation is the Greek Orthodox site of the Annunciation. Here, according to a second century Apocrypha, the angel appeared to Mary as she went to draw water at the well. A richly decorated sanctuary known as St. Gabriels' stands near the well and forms the script of the Greek Orthodox Church of the Annunciation.

St. Joseph's Church, north of the Basilica of the Annunciation, was built over a thirteenth century Crusader site marking the home of Joseph.

Gathheffer is the birthplace of Jonah and according to Jewish tradition, the site of his tomb.

Japhia is situated near Nazareth. This was a Jewish stronghold during the Jewish revolt. James and John, the sons of Zebedee, two of the apostles, are said to have been natives of Japhia.

Sephoris is the home of Anna and Joachim and the birthplace of the Virgin Mary.

Shunem is where Elisha restored to life the dead son of his hostess, a wealthy widow.

Samaria

Samaria was established by Ormi as capital of the kingdom of Israel. Samaria fell to the Assyrian King Shalmaneser in 721 B.C., after a three-day siege, thus bringing the kingdom of Israel to an end. It was reconstructed as Sebaste and was famous for its beauty in ancient times. Samaria is the traditional burial place of John the Baptist.

Samaria is located between Galilee in the north and Judea in the south. A few kilometers before we reach Samaria, we can visit the holy place of Bethel. Here Abraham built an altar, and Jacob dreamt of the ladder ascending to heaven. It is the resting place of the ark of the Covenant. Jeroboam later erected one of two Golden Calves here.

Sychar

Jacob's well, where our Lord Jesus Christ conversed with the Samaritan women, is located in Sychar. Also in Sychar is one of the oldest synagogues of Israel and the book of Torah with its gold cover. The Torah is reserved in a special place. It can be opened only when all five rabbis who have keys are present.

Mount Garizim

Moses commanded the Israelite tribes to proclaim the blessings of the Law on Mount Garizim, which is also alluded to in Jotham's parable. Mount Garizim is sacred to the Samaritans, settlers of Assyrian origin brought to Israel to settle the land in place of the Ten Tribes of Israel exiled after the fall of the Northern Kingdom. They have evolved their own religious practices, and to this day perform sacrificial rites on the peak of Mount Garizim on the festival of Passover. Mount Garizim is the source of the waters of Jacob's well, and the waters from the well go down to the Jordan River. Mount Garizim is the holy place where the Samaritan people worship God, instead of Solomon's Temple in Jerusalem.

Caesarea

Built by Herod the Great in 20 B.C. on the site of Strato's Tower, Caesarea was an official residence of the Herodian kings. After the destruction of Jerusalem, Caesarea served as the capital of the Holy Land for almost 500 years during the Roman and Byzantine periods. Here, Peter baptized the first gentile convert, Cornelius the Centurion. Paul was imprisoned here for two years awaiting trial in Rome. The Jewish revolt of 44 C.E. had its beginning in Caesarea. According to tradition, the ten martyrs including Rabbi Akiva were put to death here after the Bar Kochiba rebellion of 132-135 C.E. Caesarea was a Crusader position captured by Sultan Beibars in 1265 and destroyed by Mamelukes in 1291.

Recently a stone inscribed with the name of Pontius Pilate was uncovered in Caesarea.

Yafo, Biblical Joffa

This ancient Egyptian and Canaanite port is rich in legend. The Mythos of Perseus and Andromeda is said to have occurred in Joffa, where Jonah boarded a ship bound for Tarshish, only to be subsequently swallowed by the whale. St. Peter stayed here in

Simon the Tanner's house and raised the child Tabitha from the dead. A Crusader stronghold, Joffa was destroyed by Napoleon in 1799 and later rebuilt by the Turks.

Until about 50 years ago, Joffa was the main port for pilgrims journeying to Jerusalem on foot, on horseback, or in carriages.

Lydda

Aeneas, the paralytic was healed here by Peter (Acts 9:32). Destroyed by Vespasian and rebuilt in the time of Hadrian as Peospolis, this is the city of St. George, said to be buried here after suffering martyrdom at the hands of the Romans in 303 C.E. Today his tomb is located here. England claimed St. George as its patron saint.

Bethlehem

Bethlehem figures prominently in both the Old and the New Testament. On her way to Bethel, Rachel, the beloved wife of Jacob, died in childbirth and was buried here. Her tomb, on the outskirts of the city, is a site of Jewish pilgrimage. When Ruth and her mother-in-law Naomi returned from Moab, they came to Bethlehem and it was here that Ruth met Boaz while gleaning in the fields. Their great son, David, was anointed King of Israel by Samuel, the prophet in Bethlehem.

According to Christian tradition, it was to David's family that Jesus was born, again in Bethlehem, to which Mary and Joseph returned because of the Roman census taking place at the time. The birth was proclaimed by the angel to the shepherds in the fields outside Bethlehem, whose surrounding area is steeped in tradition.

South of the town are three ancient pools which bear Solomon's name, although the evidence suggests that he did not necessarily build them. The nearby fort is of Turkish construction.

The Basilica of the Nativity

The Basilica of the Nativity dates from the sixth century and stands over the remains of a fourth century basilica built by Constantine. The church miraculously escaped destruction during the many upheavals that racked the area and is presently administered by various orders, Orthodox, Catholic and Armenian. Each Christmas Eve, midnight mass and liturgies are said in the church and broadcast live worldwide via satellite. The Grotto of the Nativity is situated on the lower level of the church, and a flight of steps leads from it to the Catholic Church of St. Catherine next door.

The Church of St. Catherine

This church features many chapels commemorating various saints and one grotto is said to have housed St. Jerome while he wrote the Vulgate, the Latin translation of the Bible.

David's Well

David's Well consists of three large ancient cisterns. Catacombs in the area served as burial sites for the monks of the churches in the town, and bear ancient inscriptions which are still visible.

The Milk Grotto

This grotto is located a short distance from the Basilica of the Nativity. Tradition has it that Mary's milk spilt here while she was nursing the infant Jesus, turning the rock milk white.

Herodium

This is a fortress built by Herod and is the possible site of his burial. It was a rebel stronghold after the Jewish Revolt and during the Bar-Kochba rebellion.

Marsaba

This is a monastery founded by the Ascetic, St. Sava, in 483 C.E. His relics are interred here. Marsaba has long been the center of Ascetic tradition in Israel, a tradition encouraged by its harsh desert surroundings. Women are forbidden to enter the monastery.

Shepherds' Fields

Here, according to tradition, the shepherds heard the angels' joyous announcement of the birth of Jesus.

Tekoah

This is the birthplace of Amos the Prophet. It is also the home of the wise woman who reconciled David and Absalom.

Halhul

Tradition holds that Gad and Nathan, prophets in the time of King David, are buried here.

Hebron

This is the city of the patriarchs Abraham, Sarah, Isaac, Rebbeca, Jacob and Lea. They are buried here in the cave of Machpela. Hebron was King David's capital city for a seven-year period.

St. Theodosius

Here according to tradition, the Magi rested. It is the site of a large monastery founded by St. Theodosius in 476 C.E.

Jerusalem

> *Pray for the peace of Jerusalem: they shall prosper that love thee. Peace be within thy walls, and prosperity within thy palaces. For my brethren and companions' sakes, I will now say, Peace be with thee. Because of the House of the God our Lord, I will seek thy good (Psalms 122: 6-9).*

According to tradition, Jerusalem lies at the very heart of the inhabited world. Sought after by prophet and pilgrim, king and caliph, mystic and warrior alike, Jerusalem has had a long and often turbulent history. Jerusalem was originally a fortified Jebusite city conquered by King David. Here Solomon built the first temple which was destroyed by Nebuchadnezzar in 586 B.C. It was partially rebuilt by the returning Jewish exiles under the leadership of Ezra and Nehemiah. Jerusalem was later the seat of the Hasmonean dynasty, the descendants of the Maccabees who rededicated the temple after it was defiled by the Greek ruler Antiochus IV. The Hasmoneans ruled in Jerusalem until civil war led to the eventual rise of Herod to power. With Roman backing, Herod left his mark on Jerusalem through his reconstruction of the splendid second temple and numerous other buildings. It was Herod's temple that Titus razed in 70 C.E., leaving the Western Wall intact as a symbol of the yearning of the Jews for their lost homeland. Here, on the site of the former temple, the Dome of the Rock was built some time after the Moslem conquest of the Holy Land in the seventh century. This prominent landmark stands today as do the impressive walls of Jerusalem built much later by Sultan Suleiman the Magnificent in 1562.

Jerusalem figured prominently in the annals of Jesus' ministry. Here he performed miracles, healing the blind and the lame at the temple where he disputed with the pharisees. Jerusalem is the site of the Last Supper, trial, condemnation and crucifixion as well as the burial of Jesus and His resurrection.

Unified in 1967, Jerusalem is the capital of the reborn Jewish State. Members of all creeds, faiths and religions are free to tour and worship in this Holy City. Prominent pilgrim sites in the city include:

The Cenacle. This is the room of the Last Supper, It is located one floor above David's tomb. Here the Holy Spirit appeared to the disciples on Pentecost.

The Church of the Holy Sepulcher. A complex of various chapels built on the traditional site of the Crucifixion and the Tomb of Jesus. It was here that Christ appeared to Mary Magdalene, who was the first to witness his Resurrection. Stations X-XIV of the Dolorosa, the route that Jesus took to the Crucifixion, are situated here. The fourteen stations of the Cross along the length of the Via Dolorosa mark memorable events of Jesus' passion.

The Church of Mary Magdalene. This typically Russian style church was built by Czar Alexander III in memory of his mother and contains the tombs of Russian royalty.

The Dormition Abbey commemorates the death of the Virgin Mary. The tomb is located in Gethsemane, underneath the Mount of Olives. Forty steps take one down to the Tomb. Built in 431, it was consecrated in 1910.

The Gregorian Armenian Orthodox Monastery contains a collection of Armenian manuscripts and adjoins the beautiful Cathedral of St James.

The Monastery of the Cross is in the valley of the Cross. This sixth century monastery was restored by the Crusaders and marks the site of the tree from which the Cross was made for the crucifixion.

The Garden Tomb. This is an ancient Jewish sepulcher which matches the New Testament description of the Tomb in which Jesus was buried. Some Protestants hold that this skull-shaped rock is the original site of the Tomb of Jesus, as well as of Golgotha and the Crucifixion.

Ein Karem, whose name literally means the Vineyard Spring, is the traditional birth place of John the Baptist and was the site of a church bearing his name. Here, Mary of Nazareth sought out her cousin, Elizabeth, to confirm the message of the Annunciation.

Mispah marks the spot where Samuel anointed Saul as King of Israel.

Mount of Olives
New Galilee

This area is rich in historical sites including the Tombs of the Prophets, the Dominus Flevit Church, the Chapel of the Ascension and the Church of Pater Noster as well as a major Jewish cemetery. The area is at the foot of the Mount of Olives.

Gethsemane is derived from the Hebrew word for oil press and is of particular significance. It witnessed the Agony of Christ when he prayed here after learning of His betrayal. This is the site of the arrest of Christ, and of his prophecy of the Second Coming to his disciples Peter, James, John and Andrew.

Agony Church - Lord's Prayer - The Church of all Nations

This church commemorates all these events. Several nations contributed to the building of this church which was designed by Barhzzi, and which is renowned for its beauty and splendid mosaics. It contains a segment of the Garden of Gethsemane. According to tradition, the eight ancient olive trees to be found here are so old that they beheld Christ at prayer. The Grotto of Gethsemane, where the disciples would often meet with Jesus, is located nearby in the Church of Mary's Assumption which contains the Tomb of the Virgin. This church stands next to a fifth century Byzantine shrine. The Church of Agony was built in 1925, in the middle of the Garden of Gethsemane. On the top of the church are five domes. Two domes in the east site, and three in the back. Of the two, one is for Catholics and the other is for the Orthodox. The three in the back area are reserved for the Armenians, one for the Protestants and the last is for all faiths.

New Galilee

On the top of the Mount of Olives, or New Galilee, we can see and visit the Church of the Appearance. This is the church where Jesus appeared to his disciples after His Resurrection and said to them, "Peace be with you." This is also the location where

Patriarch Athenagoras and His Holiness Pope of Rome Paul the VI met and exchanged the kiss of love and forgiveness in 1967.

Not very far from this church is the Chapel of St. Thomas, who after he touched the side of our Lord, said, "My God and my Lord." Another historic church is the Church of the Lord's Prayer, or the Church of the Pentecost. Lord's Prayer because all around the walls is written the Lord's Prayer in several languages. Pentecost because on the day of Pentecost the Holy Spirit came and blessed the disciples and gave them the authority to go and teach all nations the word of God. The Mount of Olives also is the place where our Lord Jesus taught us how to pray when He said, "When you pray, pray as follows, Our Father Who art in Heaven, etc."

Underneath and not very far is the hill of the Ascension in Bethany from which Jesus ascended to heaven. It is also the Tomb of Absalom.

Emmaus

On the road of Emmaus, Jesus appeared to two of His disciples who were grieving over this death. He accompanied them to the house of Cleopas, one of the two, where He revealed himself as the Resurrected Lord.

Sephoris

This is the home of Anna and Joachim, and the birthplace of the Virgin Mary.

Jericho

Jericho is about 750 feet below sea level. It is also the oldest city in the world and the first to be conquered by the Israelites after they entered the Promised Land (I Joshua 6:20). This is the site of Joshua's dramatic conquest when the city walls collapsed at the sound of the trumpets. Jesus visited this city of Palms as a guest of Zacchaeus when Jesus saw him on a sycamore tree and had dinner with him. The sycamore tree is still in preservation for historical purposes. Nearby is the Greek Orthodox Church of St. Gerasimos. In Jericho, Jesus restored the sight of the blind man Barthimaeus.

Not far from Jericho is the Jordan River where Jesus was baptized by John the Baptist (Mark 1:9). The Jordan River is 137 kilometers long. Beginning in the Sea of Galilee, it ends at the Dead Sea.

Jericho is well known for the bitter drinking waters. "The people from Jericho went to speak to the Prophet Elisha. When they met him they said, 'Behold, we pray thee, the situation of this city is pleasant, but the water is bad and the ground barren.' Elisha went forth unto the spring of the waters, and cast the salt in there and said, I have healed the waters; there shall not be from thence any more death or barren land, so the waters were healed unto this day" (2 Kings 2:21).

Central to Jericho is the Mount of Temptation, overlooking the city. After His baptism, Jesus went to the mount and he was tempted by satan for forty days and nights without eating or drinking. "And Jesus being full of the Holy Ghost returned from Jordan, and was led by the Spirit into the wilderness. Being forty days tempted by the devil, and in those days he did nothing; and when they were ended, he afterward hungered" (Luke 4:1-2).

Between Jericho and Jerusalem is the fountain of the Good Samaritan (Luke 10:33-35).

Bethany is the home of Lazarus, Mary and Martha. It is intimately associated with scenes of the last days of the life of Jesus. The Church of Lazarus, which commemorates the resurrection of Lazarus is to be found here, as is his Tomb. Nearby is also the Church of the Meeting, where Martha went and met Jesus. "Martha as soon as she heard that Jesus was coming, went and met him" (John 11:20).

The Dead Sea

The Dead Sea is not very far from Jericho. It is long, 21 kilometers wide and 400 feet deep. The water contains 35 percent salt. The Dead Sea is the lowest spot on earth. It is 1,200 feet below sea level. The Dead Sea Scrolls, a Hebrew manuscript discovered after 2,000 years, was found nearby in the caves of Qumran.

Qumran was the center of the sect of the Essenes and the site of an Essene monastery destroyed by the Romans in 67 C.E. The renowned Dead Sea Scrolls were discovered here in 1947.

Bethabara is an ancient fort over the Jordan River where according to tradition, John the Baptist baptized Jesus.

Masada. This mountain top palace and fortress originally constructed by Herod the Great witnessed one of the most dramatic events in Jewish history following the fall of Jerusalem 70 C.E. Jewish Zealots captured the fortress which they converted into a place of refuge for survivors fleeing the destroyed capital. For two years the rebels used Masada as a base for continual harassment of the Roman forces. In 72 C.E., Governor Flavius Silva besieged Masada and in 73 C.E. its walls were breached. On the first threat of capture, Elazar, the Zealot leader of Masada exhorted its 960 Jewish defenders to commit suicide rather than be enslaved by the Romans.

Damascus Gate. Jesus entered the city of Jerusalem through the Gate of Damascus. As they heard Jesus was coming, people took branches of palms and went forth as they cried out, "Hosanna; blessed is the King of Israel" (John 12:12-14). Near the Damascus Gate is the Garden Tomb, venerated by some as the site of Golgotha.

On the outskirts of Jerusalem is **Ein Karem**, traditional home of Mary's cousin Elizabeth and the birthplace of John the Baptist. Mary's visit to her kinswoman took place here (Luke 1:39). Inside the Damascus Gate begin the steps known as the steps or stations of Dolorosa. They are the steps our Lord Jesus Christ walked with his Cross to be crucified in the place called Golgotha.

History Unrolled

The Dead Sea scrolls, discovered at Qumran, are now housed in the Shrine of the Book, part of Jerusalem's Israel Museum.

Last Visit

After the Garden of Gethsmane, the Church of Agony, the Brook of Kedron, the Tomb of the Virgin

Mary, we visited the Mount of Zion and the Upper Room the place where our Lord Jesus Christ ate his last supper with his disciples and commanded them saying, "Do this in remembrance of me. This is a Sacrifice. This is a Communion. This is a Thanksgiving. Take and eat. Drink of it all of you" (Matt. 26:26 and 1 Cor. 11:24-26).

From the Upper Room, we visited the West Wall. The day we were there the Jewish people celebrated the Sunday of Pentecost.

In the afternoon, we went back to the Holy Sepulcher to pay our respects to Golgotha and the Crucifixion of our Lord. A few steps down, we stopped at the place of the removal of Christ from the Cross (Apokathylosis). From there we went into the Holy Tomb of Christ. We made our offerings and prayed to God to forgive our sins. We lit our candle. From the Grave of Christ, we went to the Church of the Resurrection, built by St. Helen.

Before we left the Holy Sepulcher, we all bought our Savano or shroud.

The last thing to do was to go to the market and purchase our souvenirs and eat our last lunch in Jerusalem.

Late in the afternoon, some of our members left for the airport because they had to return to America, and some of us stayed for the next morning to leave Tel Aviv for Athens, Greece.

We all express our thanks to our spiritual leader Fr. George Scoulos for his efforts to organize such a beautiful tour to the Holy Land. Our ten days were pleasant, full of happiness and the services of the Jewish government were excellent.

So our tour to the Holy Land in May 1993 came to an end and I am very thankful to my Lord Jesus for making me worthy to walk in His footsteps.

Historical Narration of Jerusalem

Jerusalem was conquered by David about 1,000 C.E. It is the site of Solomon's first temple, destroyed by Nabuchadnezzer and rebuilt by Ezra and Nehemiah. Herod beautified the second temple which was destroyed by Titus in 70 C.E., leaving only the Western Wall, Jewry's holiest shrine. Jesus' ministry in Jerusalem was marked by miracles at Bethesda and Bethany, clashes with the Pharisees, the triumphal entry during Passion Week, the Last Supper in the Upper Room, the trial, the condemnation, the bearing His Cross on the Via Dolorosa, the crucifixion, the burial and resurrection, and Pentecost when the Holy Spirit descended on His followers in the Upper Room.

Jerusalem was rebuilt by the Romans after Bar Kochba's revolt at Aelia Capitolina. It was conquered by Moslems in 632, when they built the Dome of the Rock on the site of the temple. It was stormed by the Crusaders in 1099 and retaken by Saladin in 1187.

The old city walls in their present form were built by Suleiman the Magnificent. Capital of Israel. Focal point of Judaism and Christianity. Holy to Moslems. That is Jerusalem.

Jerusalem: Land of Israel. Crossroads of continents and ancient civilizations, land of the Bible and cradle of the three great monotheistic religions. This is the Holy Land for Jews, Christians and Moslems. For all who visit Israel, it is a journey back into their faith. Wherever you set foot, you are stepping on ground with Biblical associations, perhaps on the site of some great event that helped to shape history.

Jerusalem: Land of Patriarchs, buried in Hebron; of Moses, who on Mount Sinai received the Ten Commandments, the basis of a universal moral code; of Elijah, who confronted the idolaters on Mount Carmel, and of Isaiah and Jeremiah, and the other prophets who spoke the Word of God. It is the land of the kings of Israel, David, who made Jerusalem his capital; Solomon, his son, who built the first temple.

Jerusalem: Land of Jesus. Bethlehem, where He was born, and where on Christmas Eve, the midnight service in the Church of the Nativity built above the Sacred Manger takes its most meaningful form. Nazareth, Cana, Mount Tabor, the River Jordan, the Sea of Galilee with Tabgha and Capernaum, and the Mount of the Beatitudes. And finally, the culmination of it all, the core of the Holy Land, the eternal city of Jerusalem, encompassing the Church of the Holy Sepulcher and the Garden Tomb, Via Dolorosa, the Garden of Gethsemane. The Mount of Olives offers the best view of the city. It is closely connected with the last years of Jesus' life. On the slope of the mountain is the Garden of Gethsemane and the Basilica of the Agony, the Church of all Nations. On the summit of the mountain is the Church of the Ascension and at its foot, the Tomb of the Virgin Mary, where she was laid to rest before her Assumption. West of the Temple Mount of Zion is the site of the traditional Tomb of King David. And on Mount Moriah, the Temple Mount, stand two of

Islam's most Holy Shrines, the Dome of the Rock and the Mosque of El Aqsa and the Judaism's holiest shrine of all, the Western Wall, all that remains of the Temple.

Archaeological

Remains throughout the country bear witness to its glorious and stormy history and to the domination of successive conquerors. Biblical, Hellenistic and Roman cities, impressive second and third century synagogues and Byzantine churches with fine mosaic floors, Crusader towns and fortresses, Ottoman walls and the Dead Sea scrolls, a Hebrew manuscript discovered after 2,000 years in the caves of Qumran.

Throughout the ages, with the Bible in their hands, the faithful have come here from the four corners of the world to see it all with their own eyes, to worship in the very places where it all began. It was not always easy. Travel conditions were bad, and the country, at times, was desolate and even closed to pilgrims.

Today they come in multitudes. Israel welcomes the pilgrim of every faith, giving him free access to the holy shrines and providing all the creature comforts necessary for an enjoyable visit. This ancient country is at the same time a young state boasting advanced scientific institutions, universities, and cultural centers, modern cities, Jerusalem, the capital; Tel Aviv, the bustling metropolis; Haifa, the main port and industrial center; Mediterranean, Tiberias and Zefat in Galilee, spas of international repute on the Sea of Galilee and the Dead Sea, the lowest spot on the earth; and throughout the country examples of that unique system of communal living, the Kibbutz.

With a few hours you can reach any spot in the country, on good roads and by many types of transport. Accommodations include hotels, camp sites, and Christian hospices of various denominations.

Israel offers variety in everything, changing landscapes, contrasting climates, a multitude of languages. All these add to the rich experience of a pilgrimage to the Holy Land.

Part Ten

Conclusion and Sources

After the explanation of the history of the Eastern Orthodox Church we find that the Orthodox faith is not a religion that came to the world recently, but is an original form beginning from the establishment of Christianity in the world.

It is an Apostolic faith with Jesus Christ as its founder. It is a Holy Catholic and Apostolic Church without any changes or additions since the days of the apostles.

Therefore, it is right for the Eastern church to proudly use the word, Orthodox.

Sources

My sources in this presentation were the Old Testament, the New Testament, Ecclesiastical history, Byzantine history, the Liturgy, the two Encyclopedias Britannica and Americana, Xenophon's Anabasis, the Homeric Poet, Pausanias, geographer and archaeologist, 130-180 A.D., my personal research in the libraries of Lisbon, Portugal, one of the largest libraries of the world, the library in Vatican City, the Hebrew library in Shihar, Samaria, and libraries visited during my trips to Greece and other nations in 1955 and 1964.

Closing Prayer

Everyday will I bless Thee, and I will praise Thy name, forever and ever, Amen (Psalm 145:2).

By Rev. George Thomas (Thomopoulos), Tulsa, Oklahoma, U.S.A..

Dedication

I dedicate this book to my beloved spiritual children, to whom I taught the Greek language and the Orthodox Christian religion.

Part Eleven

Photographic Section

Section One:
Holy Land, June 1955

Section Two:
A Pilgrimage to Holy Land.
May 1993, Sea of Galilee

In the Footsteps of Jesus

Tiberias

Tulsa, Oklahoma.
1995 - 1996

By the Very Rev. George Thomas (Thomopoulos)

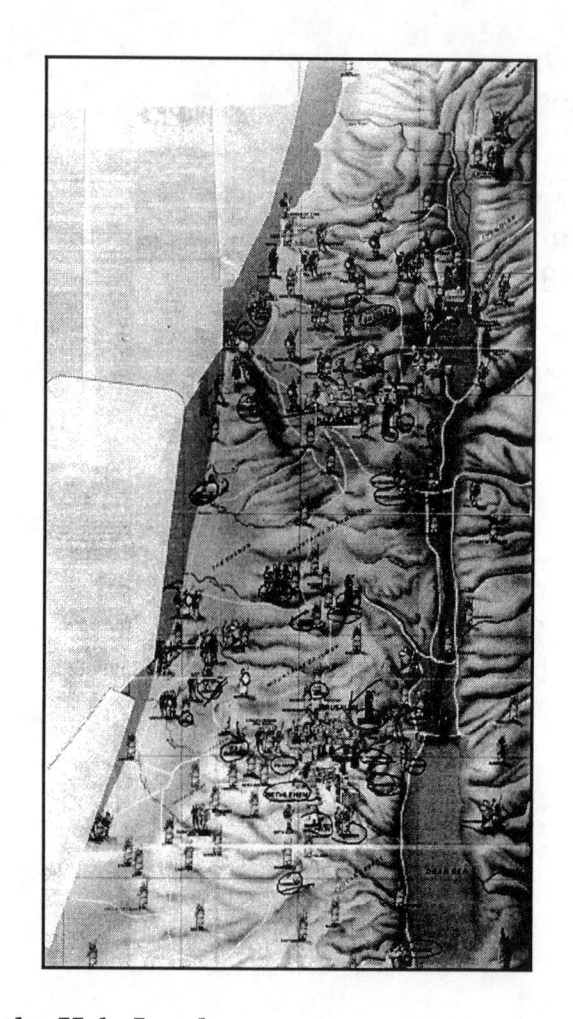

Map of the Holy Land.

Bethlehem. Church of the Nativity

Shepherd's Field

Jordan River

Mount of Temptation, near Jericho.

The fountain of the Good Samaritan. Fr. Constantine Lefteris and Fr. G. Thomas.

The Sycamore tree.

Gethsemane, entrance to the Tomb of Virgin Mary. Built in 481 A.D.

Garden of Gethsemane. Fr. Vasilios Baltsos.

Church of Agony, Lord's Prayer, in the middle of the Garden of Gethsemane. Roman Catholic. Built in 1925. Domes of all Faiths.

General view of Jerusalem from the Mt. of Olives, New Galilee

Damascus Street. Front, the Tomb of King David.

Part of the Solomon Square.

The Crucifixion of Our Lord. Golgothas.

The exterior and main entrance to the Tomb of Christ.

The Holy Grave of our Lord Jesus Christ.

The Resurrection. Christ is Risen. Christos Anesti.

Chapel of the Appearance of our Lord. Saint Thomas. On top of the Mount of Galilee.

The Ascension Hill in Bethany. The Temple of the Ascension. Fr. Baltsos.

The Church of Pentecost, or Lord's Prayer. All around on the walls is written the Lord's Prayer in several languages. Mt. of Olives.

A commemorative picture in front of the Holy Grave with his Eminence Metropolitan Derkon. Mine was destroyed in 1984.

Samaria. City of Sychar. The belfry. Monastery of St. Fotini, the Samaritan Woman. In the back is Mt. Garizim.

The chapel of Jacob's well, the source of waters from Mt. of Garizim which ends at the Jordan River.

Another view of the Holy Grave of our Lord.

Farewell. Jerusalem. Fr. George Thomas, Fr. Vasilios Baltsos, and Fr. Constantine Lefteris. 1955.

1993
Embarkation.
Fr. George Thomas (Thomopoulos) on the ship.
Epibibasis Epi Tou Ploiou 1993.

A. The Sea of Galilee
B. The Capernaum Synagogue
C. Mosaics from the Church of the Multiplication of the Loaves

A. Ein Karen. Chapel of the Beatitudes
B. The city of Ein Karem
C. The old port of Caesarea

A. Mosaic of the Multiplication
B. The Garden Tomb
C. The Via Dolorosa

A. The Synagogue Church, Nazareth.
B. The City of Nazareth
C. Mount Tabor, the Church of the Transfiguration

A. Bethlehem - Grotto of the Nativity
B. The Shepherd's Field
C. The Church of Agony, in the Garden of Gethsemane

A. Model of Herod's Temple, Jerusalem
B. The Holy Sepulchre Church
C. The Western Wall

The Dome of the Rock. Built by Abdel Malik in 691 C.E.

The Church of Saint George in the city of Cana of Galilee.

The original Tomb of St. George in the Monastery of St. George in Lydda.

The Sycamore Tree in Jericho and the Church of St. Gerasimos.

General view of Jerusalem from the Mount of Olives.

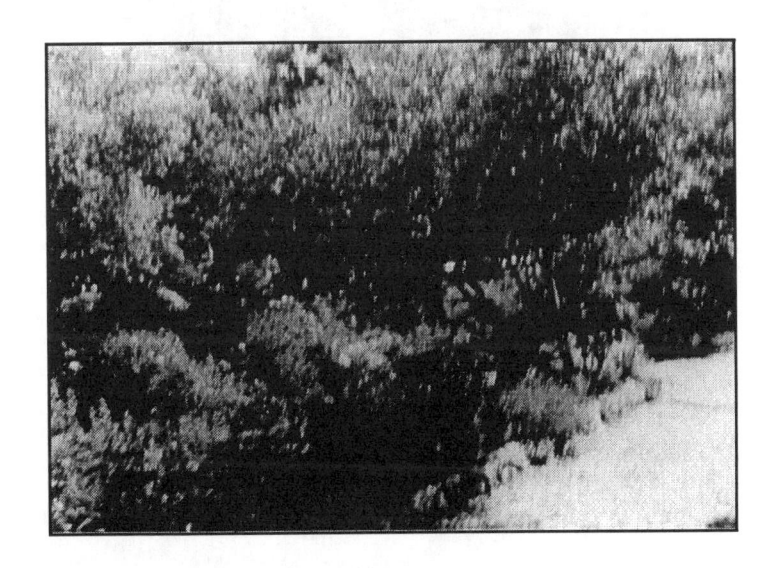

Part of the Garden of Gethsemane.

The Crucifixion of our Lord. Golgothas.

The Tomb of our Lord Jesus Christ.

Holy Temple from where the Angel announced the Resurrection of Our Lord to the Myrophores.

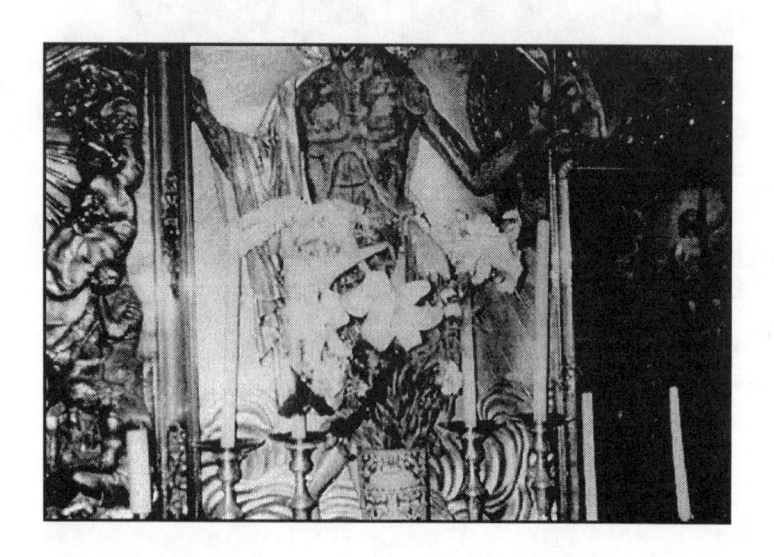

The Resurrection of our Lord. Christ is Risen - Christos Anesti

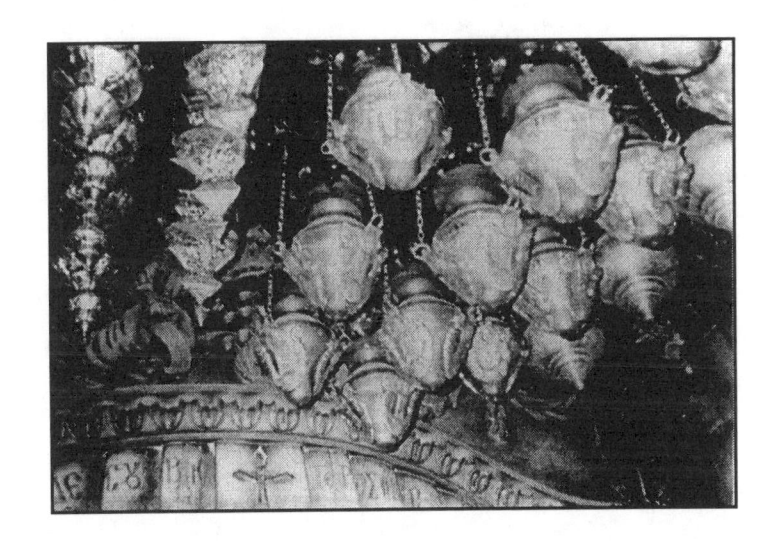

Twelve votive lights above the Holy Grave representing the Twelve Disciples.

Holy Chapels of different faiths.

A commemorative picture of our groups in front of the main entrance to the Tomb of the Virgin Mary in Gethsemane.

A commemorative picture with the Metropolitan Basilios Baltsos. Fr. George Scoulas and Fr. George Thomas.

The motel where we stayed overnight.

A small village in the desert, near the Monastery of St. Catherine. Mount Sinai.

Shopping center of the village in front of the mountain range of the Mount of Sinai.

The Garden of the Monastery of St. Catherine's.

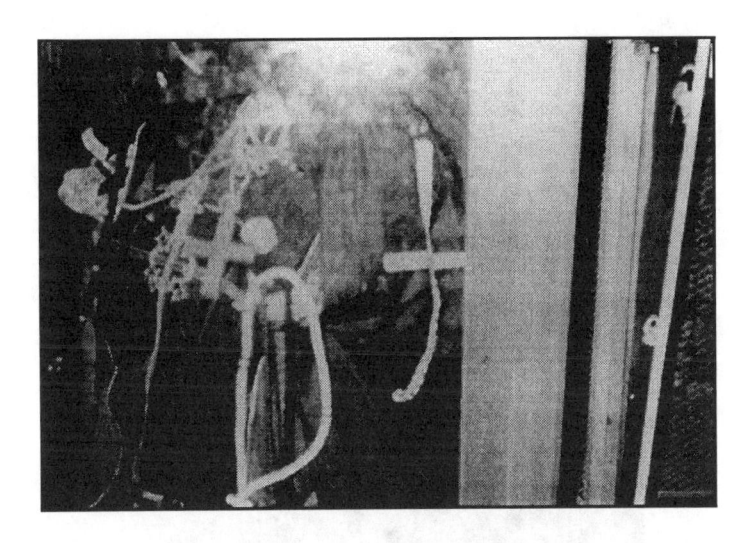

Icon of an unknown saint in the crucible where the bones of all the deceased are preserved.

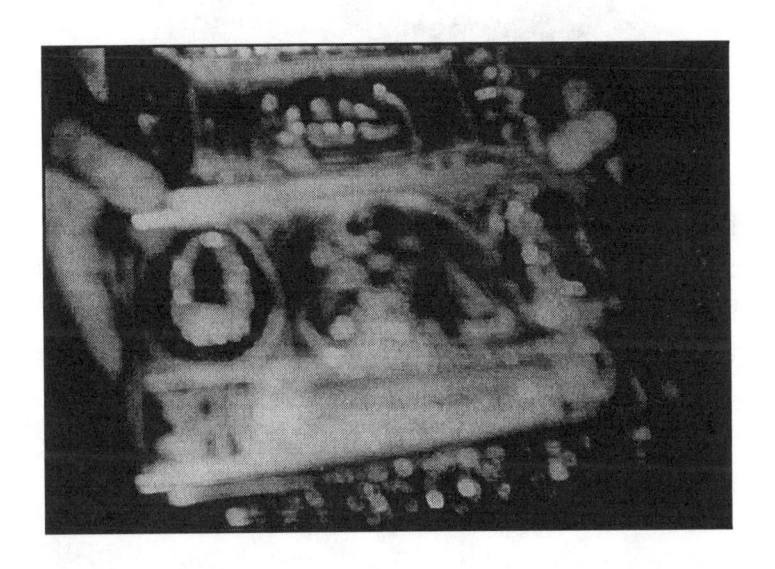

A silver box where the relics of St. Catherine "Agia Leipsana" are preserved.

A. The holy summit where Moses received the Ten Commandments from our Heavenly Father.
B. The chapel where the faithful stop and pray.
C. Mount Sinai. 1000 steps to the top. The mountain is 2,640 meters high. 1993.

His Holiness, the Patriarch of Jerusalem Diodoros, and an official certificate of our pilgrimage to the Holy Land. 1993.

A sketch of all Christian churches of the world and their separation from each other.

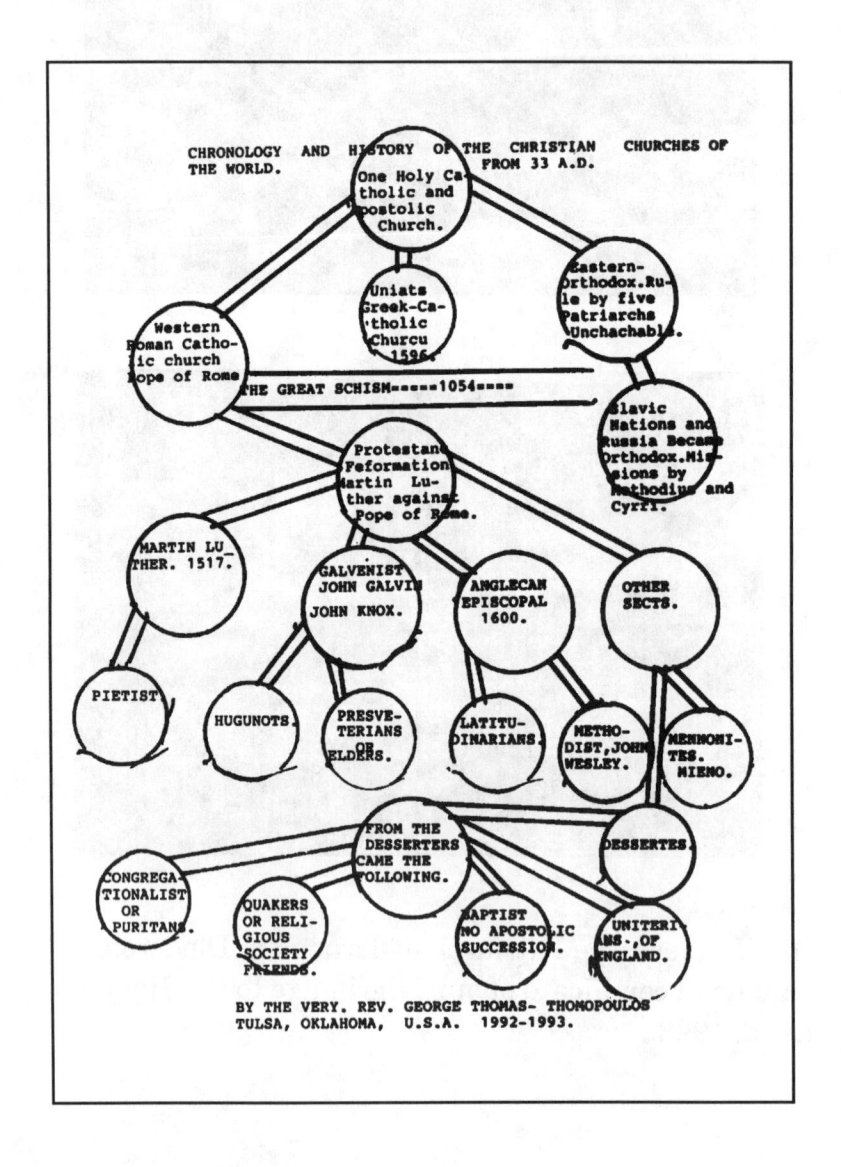

CHRONOLOGY AND HISTORY OF THE CHRISTIAN CHURCHES OF THE WORLD. FROM 33 A.D.

- One Holy Catholic and Apostolic Church.
- Uniats Greek-Catholic Churcu 1596.
- Eastern-Orthodox. Rule by five Patriarchs Unchachable.
- Western Roman Catholic church Pope of Rome
- THE GREAT SCHISM-----1054----
- Slavic Nations and Russia Became Orthodox. Missions by Methodius and Cyril.
- Protestant Reformation Martin Luther against Pope of Rome.
- MARTIN LUTHER. 1517.
- CALVENIST JOHN CALVIN JOHN KNOX.
- ANGLECAN EPISCOPAL 1600.
- OTHER SECTS.
- PIETIST
- HUGUNOTS.
- PRESVETERIANS OR ELDERS.
- LATITUDINARIANS.
- METHODIST, JOHN WESLEY.
- MENNONITES. MIENO.
- FROM THE DESSERTERS CAME THE FOLLOWING.
- DESSERTES.
- CONGREGATIONALIST OR PURITANS.
- QUAKERS OR RELIGIOUS SOCIETY FRIENDS.
- BAPTIST NO APOSTOLIC SUCCESSION.
- UNITERIANS-, OF ENGLAND.

BY THE VERY. REV. GEORGE THOMAS- THOMOPOULOS TULSA, OKLAHOMA, U.S.A. 1992-1993.